FREE

FREE
FULL RELEASE TO EVERLASTING ETERNITY

VERSALLE

To order additional copies of this book, contact:
Xlibris
1-888-795-4274
www.Xlibris.com
Orders@Xlibris.com
817120

Author's Note

Writing is freedom and therapeutic for me. This book is put together based on my deepest emotions and life experiences in the form of poetry. Poetry writing has helped me through some of my most difficult times in life. I never knew I could put words together let alone, put a book together. In this book the reader may find some unfriendly language, but as I said I am allowing people to see my deepest emotions and the different stages I have encountered in my life. The purpose is to hopefully move and motivate someone to find a positive outlet to release their deepest pain, love and emotions. Maybe one of my pieces will let someone know that they are not alone in this world, or they may relate to the love I have encountered in life. There is always someone out there going through what you are going through, especially a woman who may look like me or come from where I come from. One may find themselves in worse situations that I may have faced, but I want them to never give up and know there is always hope.

Shelton, Versalle
FREE Full Release to Everlasting Eternity

In Memory of My Loving Dad Willie F. Shelton

In honor of Love, Peace and Freedom of Speech

Contents

Snow White

Snow White came into my life just when I was a small girl
trying to figure out wrong and right in this dark space called the world
So light, so bright, so beautiful, never would I think you would steal my life
like a thief in the night
No Stars, no moonlight, no blue sky, just darkness over consuming me
and taking each breath
I sit anxiously waiting for you to take me to my peaceful place of eternity
or death

Snow White will take you in a dark place, she will lock the shackles
on real tight
while anticipating you put up an unbeatable fight
You become cold and numb wishing that this feeling will never be done

Fight for life, fight for your life, go and fight for your life
Stop giving in and don't make this Bitch your wife
Snow White she will have you fooled, making you feel amazing and good
superman I am, yeah superman I am, I can fly
Snow White is one lifelong lie
Keep following Snow White, surely, slowly and suddenly your ass will die

Snow White is not her real name some call her cocaine
Snow White may sound innocent, but will make you insane
My advice to you would be to tell this evil powder substance
Good Bye for Life

True Confession:
*I dedicate this to all of my people who battle with addiction. I myself have
never been addicted to any drug, but I have watched my family members
suffer and this is what I imagine it felt like. I have worked with individuals
who suffered from addiction and come to the conclusion that addiction is*

definitely a horrible disease. Yes, one may choose to pick up a substance and use trying to escape what inside darkness and pain they are dealing with, but I don't believe that one chooses to become an addict. May the day come that we stop judging individuals and find a solution to this horrible "epidemic" which was only identified as such when drugs began to hit suburban locations. Drugs have always played a tremendous role in my community and in my home. I feel the pain of others and wish I had the answers for them to escape this horrible world and the pain that they are in, but I don't. I can only tell you what keep me going the opposite way of drugs and alcohol and that is my Love for God and understanding my purpose on this earth. God gave each of us a talent and it is up to us to tap into it and use it for good, not to just benefit income, but growth and to help others. Find your purpose, learn it, understand it and put it to work. We are here on this planet on borrowed time and time will wait on no one, so be the best you can be and bless someone else in the mix of it all.

Peace to you Beloved

Happy Birthday

I am her and she is me
I only know how to be who God created me to be
From the beautiful smile
to the calluses under the bottom of my feet showing my miles
Happy Birthday to me

I am her and she is me
From each gray hair on my head
to the mouth that will always be fed
I am grateful for guidance and the way my life is being led
Happy Birthday to me

I am her and she is me
God granted me this life to be the best I can be
God placed me here for a purpose and a plan
I didn't always see it in the palm of my hand
Looking for love and could never understand
how this space and place was bigger than man
Happy Birthday to me

I am her and she is me
There is no other person that I would want to be
Shy little girl blossoms to a strong, beautiful woman
Walking and strolling through the world as if nothing is wrong
Learning to love and live this life until God calls me home
Grateful for every second, moment and day
Knowing and learning not to have it any other way

Happy Birthday to me

True Confession:

Life is always worth celebrating not just on your Birthday, but each and every day that is given. I have heard people say "I am not making a big deal out of my birthday, it is just another day" I really don't see it that way. We have been given a special day and time that is designated to just us. Yes, there may be someone who shares that same date, but please acknowledge your own day and know that aging is a beautiful thing. God's grace I am here and understanding my purpose!

Love Without Making Love

Heart racing, running faster than my body can understand
Butterflies in my belly, tickling my insides
leaving a warm sensual, sexy, yet settle sensation
Never leaving my body and never being touched by the hand,
but minds intertwined from the connection of our souls,
projecting an energy that only one can dream of...

This feels good and it feels so right,
never wanting to leave or end the night.
No bodies pressed against one another,
No bodily exchange of Love juices
No pressure swelling on the inside
or spreading those hips nice and wide
Just the words spoken soft and sweet
the stare that turned so quickly into a romantic glare

The way you run your fingers through my hair
Love Without Making Love
It's what I fell for, without him touching me
Love came straight from his poetic energy
Love is what allows me to be Free
Me Loving you and you Loving Me....

I Love you TY

True Confession:
Falling in Love is a Beautiful thing that should be embraced. I never thought after divorcing twice and jumping into a rebound relationship, that I would find my true soul connecting Love. I know what you are saying, so she was married twice and was not in love? The answer to that is yes I Loved him, but I was not in deep Love with him, I was in love with the

idea of having someone to be in love with me as much as I am with them. Basically, I settled for what was familiar to me, without truly finding out what he really wanted or who he really was. I ignored so many signs of a possible failure of a marriage.

This Poem was influenced by someone who I am truly in Love with and have been for the past 30 years, but life took me in another direction which I am grateful for. I believe it is safe to say that he is in Love with me also. He gave me this title and asked me to write about it and all I could do was think of him in the process of writing. I was ready to give up on finding my true Love, someone who I can grow old with and one who have an understanding and passion for Love as I do. The Universe (GOD) has brought us right back to each other. I am guessing this is our time and we needed to evolve and go through life to bring each other what we both need, honesty, respect and loyalty to one another.

Driven to Love

First look, First Glance
This was more than one night of Romance
If I could only have one good chance
I would fulfill this yearning inside and
have a lifelong slow dance

The desire, eagerness, inclination and craving was more than just lust
It was a feeling I knew I could trust
I was driven to Love and it was an absolute must

A feeling I never wanted to end
The feeling of making this person more than just my friend
I needed him and wanted him to be in my life and to have the title Husband

I was driven to Love and believed this came from the most high up above
I know I don't have to rhyme, driven to Love have me doing it every time

Traveling down a road that is so smooth
No bumps, no bruises, just a funky groove
Driven to Love keeps me in a Spontaneous mood....

True Confession: *This is another poem inspired by my true love TY. He asked me to write on this title and again it led me to just think of him and what I felt about him in high school. As a young girl I called him my crush, but as a woman I know it was more than a crush, I was actually in love with him and was too young, or too afraid to act out on it. God's plan not mine.*

Love

I fell in Love with Love a long time ago
When I met you I knew this was a feeling
that I never wanted to let go
The warm sensation that runs through my body is
one that is not familiar but I want to know
The words that come from your eyes cause a dew between my thighs
This is such a euphoric natural high
I don't want to look back, I don't want to say goodbye

I fell in Love with Love a long time ago
Your strong but sweet scent seem to be heaven
sent and is one I can never forget
You lay your hand oh so gently on my thigh
I can't help but to want to make you my guy
This is some serious shit I will tell you no lie
You have taken me on a journey and flight that I can't deny

I fell in Love with Love a long time ago
Your tall slender, slick, yet sexy physique have a sister feeling weak
I knew from day one you were the one I wanted to know and meet
The sight of you give my heart an extra thump, an extra beat
It almost makes me want to dance and move my feet
Clear out a section and allow me to move in your direction
Just a friend is what you became to me, I lost
my crush, my dream and I won't fight
My dream of being your girl your lover
your wife was no longer a might
I now can only look at you from a distance and wish you the best
I would never come in your life to make it a mess

I fell in Love with Love a long time ago
30 years later we connect like one would never imagine or know
I am not sure how this story will end but I know
I am holding on and never letting go

Yeah I fell in Love with Love a long time ago
The Love is you!

True Confession:

I have always loved the idea of being in Love and loving that amazing person who would love me back unconditionally. That kind of Love that runs powerfully over me and I would have no worries at all about anyone being able to take it away. I fell in Love with Love when I first realized who God was and opened up my heart to him and asked him to place me where he see fit. I had a clear understanding that without God there was no me. Then as I woke up I realized a person that I called my crush was actually my Love who I fell in love with a long time ago, back in high school.

Wisdom Within

Wisdom Within, you are more than my friend.
You are my sensual, sexy, satisfying creature
that lies with me from now until then
You give me strength and power,
Power without control, but with a tower that
only my heart knows how to hold.
Wisdom Within, I dare not call you my friend.
My lover, my life, from beginning and until the end
You stood by me when I fell weak
Weak from the walls, that taste and smell oh so sweet, that are
soft and meek, that wrap around me from my head to my feet
Wisdom Within, you are more than my friend
There is never a need for me to masquerade, beguile or pretend
You see I fell in love with you way before this life begin
It took some time for me to get this all right, and
the universe knows I put up a hell of a fight
I came from a place where shit wasn't requisite or right
I traveled through that dark tunnel and
approached this thing called life
But where would I be without the strength and love of my wife

So let me show you the man that I can be
Let me show you what make me-me
Allow me to hold you up my lover and my friend
Let me introduce you to my Wisdom Within!

Dedicated to my Nephew Samuel McGill
Versalle Shelton 12/22/17

True Confession:
I did this piece as it says completely for my nephew. I have seen his growth and maturity as a man and if I could imagine him talking to his beautiful wife who has stuck by his side for the past years and have endured some challenges in the marriage, this is what he would say to her.

Search for Passion

I have searched high and low, I have been through it all,
From turtles, to frogs, even thought of collecting balls.

You promised me love until the end
When it happened I did not know where to begin

Adjustment and Adaptation like the organisms in the sea
It's not what I really wanted, but forced myself to be.

The strength, the passion, the desire, it was all there,
But in a blink of an eye, you didn't care

You walked away, and left me to die
Like the Ghost Orchid, that I could only see in the sky!

True Confession:
This was a prompt from one of my writing classes. I also have a love for Orchids!

Simple and Sweet

Yes, Simple and Sweet
Is how you seemed to be
You even told me you wanted
To marry me.
I was such a fool to believe
To believe that such a divergent
Relationship could become one
Like a cycle of clothes washed in a sweet detergent

Yes, Simple and Sweet
Is how you seemed to be
At one time I loved to hear you talk to me
What was once so sweet and I loved to have around
Quickly became so irritable and a dissonance sound
A sound like no other, where conversation, became
Arguments when we talked to each other

Yes, Simple and Sweet
Is how it seemed to be
What was once hours of conversation
Slowly became muttered words
Like a delayed train in the station.

Yes, Simple and Sweet
Is how you seemed to be
I believed you was my friend
But like a serpent, a python,
You destroyed relationships,
And bought them to an end.

Finally, after years of this big fight
I was able to see the light.
You came like a thief in the night.
The very last day you were like a snake
You left me with nothing besides a plank
Now I walk with my head held high
Wishing I didn't wait so long to say goodbye.

I sit and I laugh and now I see
that life is really simple and sweet,
Because I know how to love God and Me.

True Confession:

Sometimes we have to go through something to get somewhere. This was my journey of searching for a love that was not real and I allowed myself to be used. I realized I needed for this to happen so that I could realize who God is and how much I needed him in my life. As it says in the end I was so happy in the end to be rescued from an unhealthy relationship. The lesson learned, is to always keep God first.

Tool

Screwdriver, Wrench, Hammer,
You think you have the right tool
But please, oh please, you are looking like a fool.

I was one to always play by the rules,
And only could hope that you had
the right tools.

See a lot of us do become fooled
because it feels right, we think this is amazing
and want to work on it all night

Sexy, seductive, and sensual, you seem to be,
Oh please don't drop those loose screws on me!

I am one from the old school,
So don't think for one minute you have me fooled.

Mamma told me about men like you,
The one who will come to help,
but really don't know what to do.

I see it like this, if you have the
right tools, then maybe I could be fixed.
Put me together nice and tight, and then
I could be yours for the rest of your life!

True Confession:

So many times we hear of a man thinking with his penis and there are times when women fall for all of this. There are times when the flesh can take completely over and we forget who we really are and our value as humans (woman and men). A man need to know that he is much more than his tool he carries and the way to a woman's heart is not between her legs. We can build each other up and have a long lasting lifetime relationship, if we stop focusing on the flesh and allow our inner self to take full control. Side note: It took me a very long time to learn this. I could have not done it without having a connection to a higher power. Meditation led to Motivation.

Let's Do It Again

When we met, some may say it was not right,
When we met it was supposed to go no further than that night.
When we met it seemed like it was meant to be.
I thought I could be your friend, but knew that this soon would come to an end.

Deep in my heart I knew it was not right, but I was too caught up to give up the fight.
What was ever so wrong, felt amazingly so right!
I was selfish and wanted to have it all, you, me, and he! Aw Man, how could this be?
How could I be with someone who was not for me?
How could I look him in the eyes and say I love him, when my heart is really not with him?
One night turned into what seemed like a lifetime! I lost you for some years, but never lost you in my mind.
What was at one-time lust, became my biggest fear,
the fear of Love, but I could not Love you right here!

Finally, I find my friend, and I want the chance to do it again!
I want to start over the right way, I want to know your mind, body and soul!
Let's do it again.
This time we don't meet in a club, but our hearts dance to the same beat.
The beat of God's word and his Love!
I want to be able to know when you need a kiss and a hug!
I want to be there for you in every way that I can, I want to be your woman and you my man!
I want you to be able to tell me how this story will end, and I say please let's do it again!

True Confession:

Once again, I was looking for Love in all of the wrong places. I know exactly who I was with and who I was talking about it this poem. I will not share any names, but I will say I was in a marriage at one time in my life and did not want to be there. The biggest mistake of my life was cheating and looking for something in someone else, who was really not for me. My pain was personal and I needed to fix that before I could move on. Out of this came my first divorce and a broken home, but a sense of relief knowing that I would not hurt someone that I cared about and to give him the opportunity to find true Love that he could not find in me and I could not find in him. Then I went backwards and reconnected with the person who I met years ago in a club, and we all know that is a failure waiting to happen. Never go back! Needless to say that didn't work out too well and I ended up with me, myself and I.

Free

This sparrow represents me, because I am free!

This sparrow represents me, because the shackles have been loosened mentally!

This sparrow represents me, because I have flown through fire, felt the pain, even been burned, but, I am still free!

This sparrow represents me, because sometimes it gets a bit cloudy, but I am still able to see and be free!

This sparrow represents me, and this is who I strive to be, A free loving woman!

This sparrow represents me, I am free to Love, I don't have a blocked artery or cloudy mind, I am free to Love God and humanity! I am Just Free to Be Me! This is my story!

True Confession:

Doing this small piece was an introduction of who I had become over the years. Many had asked me the question "was my tattoo pertaining to my divorce from my husband", well since I had been divorced for 5 years prior to getting this tattoo, the answer was clearly NO! I would never look at my marriage as something I was locked in or forced to be in, I was there by choice. The bird on my back is a Sparrow, this particular bird represents Love. I put the word FREE on the bird, because he represents the freedom I have to Love and connect with God. The bird is flying through a dark cloud, which represent me going through certain struggles in life.

No Rhyme No Reason

No Rhyme No Reason, I just say what's on my mind.
You call me aggressive, because I won't allow you to disrespect me.
I won't allow you to take me way back into history!
Yeah, His Story that's what it is when you look at me,
Not my story but, what you think you can see in me!

No Rhyme, No Reason, I just say what's on my mind.
I won't allow you to get into my space and you damn sure
better back the hell up out of my face!
You see there is a lot of shit that need to be let go,
but every time I see you, I hear you, or I smell you,
it's all regurgitated right back in my esophagus again, because I am
trying so hard to hold it in.
So I let it go, I just say what's on my mind, without any reason, or rhyme!

You say you understand, but I know you could never understand,
Your mind has been shaped and molded to believe about me what you
see on TV.
But let me tell you, I am not a star, I am not famous, I am just a child
of God!
A child who is free to say what's on her mind, without any reason or rhyme!
And if you ask me to, I can't spit something at you with the drop of a dime!

True Confession:
Honestly speaking I am not sure what triggered this particular piece, but I can say it may have come from simply living in a world as a Black woman and always being judge by the color of my skin. It does not matter to some, how far you have come, or how hard you have worked, or how hard you love humanity, in their eyes you are still portrayed as someone less than. Someone may have said something to me or I may have read something that happened to a person of color, non the less, this is my reality.

Dancing to Your Own Beat

You danced to your own beat.
I thought it was the love you had for me.
By the stench that shot out from your mouth,
I knew it was not about me.
But I still hung on and danced with you until
You could not see.

You danced to your own beat.
Even when my mother walked passed stomping her feet.
You kept the shuffle going,
Even without thinking and knowing.

You danced to your own beat.
While one hand held on to me,
The other swung but it missed me.
I would not believe that this could be,
A man who joined in to create me,
Really did not know how to love me!

You truly danced to your own beat!

True Confession:
This may have been encouraged by a class prompt or reading, but I think when I was doing it I did think of my father. Although my Dad never ever abused me in any kind of way, he absolutely adored me, I thought of him when doing this. My Dad battled with Alcohol abuse, and always really danced to his own beat. He was a loving guy who just got caught up with trying to escape from whatever pain he was facing. My Dad had this calm and soothing voice and when he spoke to me it was never annoying but always relaxing. My Dad was the first person to teach me what Love was and what it meant to be Loved. After his death I searched so hard looking for that Love.

I've Got a Story to Tell

I've got a story to tell
I've got a story to tell
Now you may think you know this all so well,
but I will tell you how these shoes have walked through hell!
Oh yes, I have a story to tell!

I was born in the hood, and that is all good, but what happens when
you start to feel stuck, and you just want to throw up your hands and
say I really don't give a fuck!
Oh yes, I have a story to tell!

I have watched my parents come and go, and left me with so much, that
you will never know.
No its not money, or material things, but it is memories and lessons,
that I can pass on again and again!
Yes, I have a story to tell!
I have seen and lived with drugs, and thugs, and not too many damn hugs!
Oh wait I did get the hugs, but they came from the thugs.
Damn where is the real love!
Oh yes I have a story to tell!

True Confession:

*We all have a story to tell. I grew up loved in a strange way, a way that only
my parents knew how to love. Growing up poor and in restricted conditions
gave me a different kind of strength and love. As a little girl, I saw things
that no little girl should ever see, at least I know my child never saw any
of this life style. Drugs, alcohol, parties and enough food to just survive
off of. I was kidnapped by one of my cousins, well maybe not kidnapped,
handed over to her for a weekend and she attempted not to return me to
my parents, but again I had a Father who adored me. No matter what his
sickness was, he would never allow anyone to hurt me. What they didn't*

realize was how much pain was all around me and it was only the grace of God who kept me safe. I was exposed to so much by my loving parents and family remember they loved me the way they knew how. I am not taking anything away from them in raising me, but could have been better maybe or maybe not, in the end I am standing strong and I have great memories! I learned to do the opposite of everything that I saw, besides making a way out of no way and keeping my place clean. Yeah that's Love!

Wild Wild West

Here I am living in the wild wild west!
and it is truly a f@$%*ing mess!
Now I know you are saying I don't usually do this,
But you need to know when a girl is pissed,
and besides how else am I supposed to relieve my stress?

Here I am living in the wild wild west!
I walk through this world trying to be my very best,
but here you come forcing me to grow hair on my chest.
I work so hard and always pray to God, but then I turn the corner
and here is a damn fool trying to make my faith shorter.

Here I am living in the wild wild west!
Oh Yes! This place is a damn mess!
I can't walk down the street with a smile on my face,
because then you want to try to invade my space,
You really need to know when to stay in your place!

Here I am living in the wild wild west!
I keep praying to God and he keeps me focused on the best.
I know that forward is the only way for me to go,
and that he is the one who is running my show!
So even though I am living in the wild wild west!
I now understand that this is only a test!

True Confession:

Growing up in Harlem was not easy, but definitely shaped and molded me into a thick skin Black Woman. Surrounding myself around those who seem to be the best at that time. Yep, they were some of the best Drug dealing, hustling people you would ever want to meet, but it gave me a sense of being protected. Nope, many did not know my name and that was OK, but they *knew my face and respected that. Oh the lovely 80's when crack was at an all-time high and making a lot of people rich while unfortunately was killing others at the same time. I have witnessed and done things that I will not mention to condemn myself. I have affiliated with murderers and creeps who appeared to be so nice, years later I found out they were really criminals and good actors. Yes, the wild wild west it was, growing up on the west side and walking the avenue from 155th Rucker's games, Roof Top Skating Rink to Willies lounge even further down to 125th and then over to Lenox Ave. Yep my girls and I ran the streets of Harlem. Looking like some innocent females not looking for trouble but at the same time wanted all the attention from the "bad boys". Then I matured and realized it was a big freaking mess I was in and only by God's grace I still stand today.*

Love Hurt?

Just as soon as I think I have it, I want to give it up
It only feels good for a little while, even though it's said to be forever
How can you say you love me, and hurt me at the same time?
How can you say you love me, and you don't give a damn about my feelings?
How can you say you love me, and you are never with me, this is a feeling I don't like!
At times I cry myself to sleep, just thinking of what I want it to be like.
At times I smile to myself just imagining what it would be like.
Love Hurt?
I ask God to send you to me, whoever you might be.
I ask God why is this so difficult, why does it hurt.
I tell God I have now put him first, so why do I still feel this way?
Love Hurt?
How can I ever remember your smile, if I never see your face?
How can I continue to love you, if I never get to touch you?
How can I remember your scent if I never get to smell you?
How can I remember your flavor if I never get to taste you?
Love Hurt?
This is not what I want, this is not how it's supposed to be,
So I say, maybe it's not for me!
I have learned to love that other person who looks just like Vee, and
That would be me!
Love shouldn't hurt!

True Confession:
This piece describes once again How I fell in Love with Love, but Love was not loving me back, or I was just trying to share my love with all of the wrong people. I began to feel like I was getting hurt from trying so hard to find true love.

How Can I Flow!

How can I flow! The words are in my heart, but have no place to go! How can I flow! I want to be free, free to see what I really want to see, but there is something blocking my view, smearing my vision! How can I flow!

I want to move, I want to dance, but my feet won't move they are stuck, something is holding me down like two bricks cemented to the ground, damn I can't even turn around!

How can I flow!

I'm thinking, I'm getting a feeling! I pick up my pen, put it to the paper, it moves, the words are flushing and rushing out! OK! OK! Now I'm flowing!

This is just a little piece to express, how I get stuck sometimes in my writing, but I realize if I never put the pen down I will never stop writing. The key is to keep going and never ever stop!

True Confession:
This piece is self-explanatory. At times there is really a thing called writers block, and you just don't know what to write about, your thoughts may be blocked with other things in life. My advice is to try meditation and relax, then pick up that pen and get to writing. It will come right back to you.

Alone

I sit here wondering, wondering if I am afraid to be alone

Even with my friends on the outside and my family all around, I can still feel alone.

Sometimes I cry, and I look around for that healing, that someone to say it will be alright, but I am alone.

I want to scream but the words won't come out, because I know that I am alone.

What does it really mean to be alone? We say we are happy, but are we really? If you are happy, why do you date, what are you looking for?

I think you are looking for that someone special so that you won't be alone.

If you say you are happy why do you open your legs to someone that you will not marry, you allow him to enter that dark lonely hole, that hole you hope to fulfill with joy and happiness.

Is this the hole that leads to your heart? I don't think so; I'd rather be alone! I go from a Husband to a broken home, I move on to a sub to fulfill the vacancy, but that does not work, so now where am I alone!

One day I get it! I get on my knees and I pray to God, not for the right person but for him to step in and take over my life! I opened up my heart to him and he opened up my eyes!

I see, I can really see I am not alone, God is here for me and with me, he is who I cry to and he hears my cry. He is who I talk to and he tells me what to do! I have learned to move when God says to move!

I AM NOT ALONE!

True Confession:

Feeling alone and believing that another person can bring you joy is false. My belief is you have to find your own internal joy and then you will find happiness. Depression is real and will sneak up on you without you even realizing what is happening. I had to come out of my own sadness and find joy, which was not around me, but in me. I cried out to God for a healing, I kept writing and I found peace. Peace with my decisions in life, Peace with knowing that things will not always turn out the way we see fit. My marriage was not a complete failure, because I have a beautiful daughter from that relationship and I still have a good relationship with my ex-husband. I learned a lot about Love and what I really wanted to gain from my relationship. I learned who I was as a woman and my role in life as a wife. Never look at anything in life as a failure, but more of lessons learned. Honestly speaking, a person can be in a full relationship and feel lonely, so at times it may be better to be alone and not lost and lonely in a situation.

Nigger (Nigga) to WOMAN!

Yeah I was born a Nigger, but I am now a woman!

Yeah I was born in a time where we were once called Nigger Then Negro's, and now Nigga again, but I am none of the above, I am a Woman!

Yeah it's said that I am African American, but how African am I? I was born here.

Check my background and my ancestors seem to be Caucasian, or White as they say.

Yeah white meaning as written in the book, free from sin, pure. How pure is white, when white tapped into and disturbed my Black Roots?

Yeah Black as we are so proud of! Black meaning as written in the book, not hopeful, sad, dark-skinned. Now don't get me wrong, I love this chocolate caramel skin I'm in, but why do you call yourself Black again?

Yeah I was born a Nigger, but I am now a woman!

As I see it, I'm not Black or White! I am just human! A Beautiful Human Woman! Human meaning of characteristics of man; a person!

Yeah I was born a Nigger, but I am now a woman! Woman meaning an adult female human!

Yeah that's who I am, even if the constitution states I am 3/5ths of a man! A woman who fears no one but God! A woman who is free! A woman that will never bow down! A woman who will always speak her mind!

Yeah I was born a Black Nigger in your world, but this is my world now and I am A FREE WOMAN! FREE TO BE ME!

True Confession:

I was born in the early 70's and came from a mother who was given away by her mother and was raised by a White woman. This is something that stripped my mother of her culture and who she was as a black woman. My mother did not know what it was too embrace your culture and who you really were. My mother believed that dark skin was not as attractive as the lighter or brown skinned black person. My mother believed in straight hair was how your hair should be, "Nappy Hair" was not something that she tolerated. Even the softest texture of coil hair we had that was not acceptable. I never had black doll babies except for one life size doll that stayed at my Auntie Flora house and I could not play with her, because she was special. Yes, little did I know how special she really was. I remember having a whole line of white Barbie's and White Baby Alive, so embracing my culture was not something that was passed down from my home. As I became a young adult and begin to listen to my older brother, who introduced me to historical black legends like Malcolm X and the Black Panther movement, then and only then I begin to realize who I was. I still wore my hair straight for many years, even made the horrible mistake of straightening my daughters' hair. (lessons learned)

Then to live in a world that have so much racial division and so much hate for my race in particular, I had to learn to love who I was and not allow anyone to label me. Why when people look at me, they can't just see a beautiful woman? Yes, I am Black and I am proud, please don't get that twisted, but what do you see past that?

Soul Mate

I can feel your pain, when your stomach ache, my stomach ache even more...is this my soul mate?

When you lost your loved one, I felt what you were feeling deep inside as if I lost my very own blood...is this my soul mate?

I cried every night along with you, even though I was not beside you.... is this my soul mate?

I dream when you dream and we dream about the same person at the same time...is this my soul mate?

You are in my mind and complete my thought, when I speak you finish my sentence...is this my soul mate?

I cry every time I have to leave you, and I am so happy when I'm with you... You smile, I laugh, I laugh, you smile, and then we just laugh together... is this my soul mate?

You comfort me when I am in pain, you feed me when I am hungry, you rub my feet, I caress your chest, I scratch your back, I include you in my prayers before I pray for myself, I pray for the day to come, to hear those words, "will you be with me forever"....is this my soul mate?

When I am around you after so many years the feeling has never changed, it's a feeling I can't fight, and I don't want to fight....is this my soul mate?

I love you for who you are and not what you have...Damn I think he is my SOUL MATE!

True Confession:

It's funny how a person (me) can be searching for love so hard, because love is who you are and it is what you want, that you can believe a person is your soulmate. This piece is what I believe it should feel like when you do find your soul mate. During this time, I did not have a "Soul Mate" I was praying that I did. My heart was there with this person and I was in pain for them due to their loss of a loved one, but definitely souls were not connected. Yes, I care about them, because that is who I am, I am full of compassion and since I have known this person for so many years the compassion for them was that much deeper than most. Now here I am 10 years later and understanding the difference and believe that I really have met my soul mate, who I want to marry and live the rest of my life with. My belief this is a connection from God.

Why Are We So Mad?

Why do you get mad when they say "We are still their Slaves"?
Is it because it is true? Think on it for a minute, we do contain ourselves with ignorance, greed, and selfishness!
Why do you get mad when they say Ignorance is the primary weapon used against us?
Remember the person who said" The best way to hide something from Black people is to put in a book"? Oh you probably never even heard of that, because we don't pick up books!
Why do you get mad when you can't win an argument or debate logically in a conversation? You get upset when someone uses the word ignorance against you, when it simply means lack of knowledge, but your level of ignorance is so high that you did not even know that!
Why do you get mad when you walk in your community and you see all these new stores owned by someone other than you? Guess what it could have been you, had you took the time to read the local paper, or went to a community board meeting, or checked public records!
Why do you get mad, when they get you to spend all that money on people who can care less about you or your family, yeah you have, look in your closet, look at the name that is printed on those jeans, that shirt, open your eyes and take a good look.
Why do you get mad when they tell you, how you were not wise enough to take your money and invest in it, instead you went and purchased a house and a nice whip, and now you are foolish enough to believe that you have status?
You are mad at me right now for telling you about us! Free your self-people READ, EDUCATE, TEACH!
Remember we are all "Free TO Be ME"!

True Confession:

Sometimes we (People of Color) need to hear the truth and be the change in us. How can we grow as a people, when we sit and do nothing to change ourselves? This was done in mind for all of those who sit and complain but won't even attempt to change who they are. Minds have been conditioned so bad that some really believe there is no way out. Now don't get me wrong I do know that this system is not made for us, and there is no mistake how the neighborhoods are built. There are definitely disparities in the communities, but we must push and work a little harder. Expect the unexpected and do it for yourself. Push a little harder than normal. Teach your children to be better than you were. My child told us (her parents) that she was not raised poor like us, so she can do certain things different. I smiled and said "You are welcome and thank you for complementing your parents" Job well done! Read and Free your mind Beloved.

Remember (Dedicated to Evon Edwards) R.I.P.

Remember me, not for who I was, but for who I am

For I will always be with you

Remember my love that I have for you will stay in your heart for a lifetime

Remember when you think of me, only think of the good times we shared together

Remember the times we sat and had long talks

Remember the smile that was upon my face, like the sun shining in your eyes on a hot summer day

You can cry if you must, but remember after the rain flowers will blossom

Remember how I always told you "I love YOU" now take that love and share it with someone else

Remember to listen to your heart beat and you will hear my voice, you will feel my positive energy flow through your veins like streams flow through the river

Remember to be happy with the years that we shared together they may seem short, but great memories will last a lifetime

I WILL FOREVER BE WITH YOU

Remember to hold on to faith, trust, and believe in the unseen, even though you won't see my physical flesh again, I will be with you in spirit

Remember you can smile now, for I am out of pain. I am free and home with my Father!

P.S. Always remember me!

I will forever miss you Momma Evon!

True Confession:

This was a hurtful time. Losing someone in your life is never easy, but remember them how they were and allow their spirit to live through you. No she was not my biological mother, but she showed me so much love, one would think I was related to her. I will never forget how she made me feel as a person. She was always happy to see me. I cry every time I read this!

Earth Day

You cried when they gave you the word

You cried when you found out the truth

No these were not tears of joy, or fear

these were tears of I messed up again

These were the tears of unplanned decisions and disappointment

These were the tears, of you really did not want me!

Little did you know you didn't want me but God did

He did not make a mistake when he created me

Now I am here and you never say you love me
You try to show me, and I can feel it,
but could you imagine the joy that I feel if you would just say it!
Why is it so hard? Why is it so difficult?
I did not ask for this day; I did not tell you
I wanted to be here.
This is the day God created me.
This is the day that he allowed me to enter this earth
Some like to call it my Birthday, but I say this is My Earth Day!

True Confession:

I remember conversations about how my mother felt when she found out she was pregnant with me. As a mother myself, I can't imagine telling my child that I was so upset when I found out I was carrying her. Now, unfortunately my child was not my first pregnancy. I was on a horrible medication and

could not bring a child in the world that would be at a high risk for living. (God has Forgiven me). I know that I am forgiven, because I have been blessed with my daughter. At times we don't know the impact of our words especially when speaking to our children. I carried this pain for some time and finally released it on this canvas. Yes, I am still here! God is awesome!

Hands

With these hands I will protect you
With these hands I am able to hold you
With these hands I can guide you
With these hand you know that you are safe with me
These are the hands that will never touch you in the wrong way, but always at the right time
These are the hands that will wipe your tears away when they run down your beautiful cheeks
You will never have to worry when you put your hand in my hand
When I touch your hand I can feel your heart beat, I can feel the love that you have for me through these precious little hands
If you follow these hands I promise you I will lead you in the right direction
These are the hands that will see you by touch when there is no more sight
These are the hands that will love you for life!

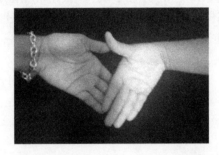

True Confession:

This is one of my favorite pieces! This shows the Love that I have for my one and only daughter! She was nothing but a Blessing to me and as I told her, I will always have her back. She is a gift from God and as long as I have breath and she does what is correct, I will be here. I will even be around when she trips and fall. I don't take any of my blessings for granted. This is actually framed in my home and I hope she will keep it for life and pass it down to her children.

Family

*F*orever loving me, through thick and thin
*A*lways having my back and knowing when to say I'm sorry or I love you
*M*eaning it when you do say you love me
*I*mmediate response when I am in need
*L*istening to my issues and not judging who I am
*Y*earning to live this life time with me, and to share many more moments together

True Confessions:
Always love your family! We don't know how long we have here on this Earth, spend
your time wisely. My Family is as close as we will get at this point in our lives. There are some who are loved from distance, due to their lack of understanding what loyalty and love is, especially within family. If any of my family is reading this, I want them to know that I really do Love them, even if we don't see or talk to each other daily my love never faded away. My dream it to have a big Family reunion and see all of my relatives, both old and new.
On another note, Family is not always your blood relatives, I have been blessed with many family members who are my friends.

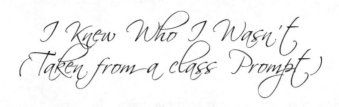
I Knew Who I Wasn't (Taken from a class Prompt)

That little girl who always wanted to hang out every week instead of going to class
Wasn't me.
That little girl who would cut school to lay up with a nigga who never even planned on finishing school
Wasn't me.
That little girl who struggled through school, the one who never enjoyed a summer because she spent it every year in summer school
Wasn't me.
That little girl who finally graduated, and went to college, but did not have a clue, she only knew how to be cute
Wasn't me.
That little girl who kept a job, but did not know what to do with her money
Wasn't me.
That little girl who spent more time on the streets with the hustlers than her own family
Wasn't me.
That little girl did not know who she was, but she damn sure know who she Wasn't!

True Confession:
This was taken from a class prompt as it says. This was when I realized that I could put words together and make some poetry art out of them. This professor would come in the class and write a few words on the board and told the class to write, move your pen and don't stop until he said to stop. I never knew I could think on that level. Non the less I did it and fell in Love with it. It made me feel good to write. This taps into my reality of coming into myself as an adult and what I went through traveling in that part of my life.

The Oppressor

I'm trying to get up, but you hold me down
It's like an elephant crushing down on my chest cavity
I'm trying to breathe, but I can't
My heart is racing faster and faster and faster, like it want to jump out
of my chest

I'm trying to get up but you hold me down
I feel like that heroin addict trying to kick a bad habit
I want to walk away, but it just keep calling me back
I have the shakes, my stomach is in knots
I can't' fight this feeling, this feeling that is ripping me apart on the inside

I'm trying to get up but you hold me down
You rule over me tyrannically, I have become your slave
I have no control over me anymore, you have my spirit trapped with
only one-way out
These shackles have me bonded, I can't move, my body feels weak like
I have the flu
I'm weak in my legs, I don't want to get up
Even when I try you still hold me down

I'm trying to get up but you hold me down
What is this? What is this thing that has me so oppressed?
This thing that has become my new master
This thing that will have you believe the only way out is death
This thing that just entered into to my soul and stole my spirit away
This damn thing called depression has been my oppressor!

True Confession:

This piece shows what one (myself) was feeling during a time of depression and not really understanding what was happening to my mind and body. Depression is real and can take control of a person in a blink of an eye. I always thought I had control of my feelings and being a believer, I never thought something like this would come my way. I was able to get through this without medication, but not without God in my life. If you are suffering with depression, please don't hesitate to reach out to someone and talk about it. It is okay we all have something going on in our lives that is hard to handle. Asking for help is a good thing, no matter who you are.

These Eyes

Tell me what do you see when you look into these eyes?
Tell me how do you feel when you look into the eyes?
Are these the types of eyes that you would be honest with?
Are these the type of eyes that you want to look back at you when you speak?
Tell me what do you see when you look into these eyes?
Tell me do you see pain in these eyes?
Do these eyes look like the kind of eyes that have seen a lot?
Tell me do you see joy in these eyes?
Do you smile when you look into these eyes?
What is it that you really see in these eyes?

I can tell you about these eyes. These eyes have shed plenty tears.
Some tears from joy, and some from pain.
These are eyes of a strong woman,
A woman who can see what direction she is going in.
These are eyes who can see a fake.
These are eyes who can see a friend.
These are the eyes that I want you to look in and see my heart.
These are the eyes that I want you to look in and see that I am Real!
These are the eyes that will watch your back.
What do you see in these eyes?

True Confession:

There are times when you develop relationships and friendships that seem to be so real and honest, then you find out that the person you trusted is really not your friend. I wish that I could look into someone's eyes and really see how true they are. I have developed over the years the capability to pick up on energy. This happened after my Spiritual growth over time. I want people to know that when they look into my eyes and hear the words from my mouth, that I am truly honest and mean what I say. I would never tell a person I love them, or care about them if it was not true. I have heard it said "your eyes are the windows to your soul" so I would hope that one sees how good my soul is when they are looking into my eyes.

Remember the Time....

What happened to the good old days?

Where have I heard this before?

Remember the time when your fam was the block?

Remember the time when everybody looked out for each other?

Remember the time when you could send your child to the store and know they would be safe?

Man what happened to those days?

Now instead of the block looking out for child, they are looking at your child, watching how nice they are growing up and out, watching to see when the time is the right time!

What in the hell happened to the good old days?

The days when we could trust Mr. Charlie, or Ms. Loula Mae.

Remember the time when you could sit in the house and keep your door open?

Remember the time when you knew every single neighbor by first name?

Remember when people would say Good Morning to each other on the elevator?

Remember when you could go to your neighbor's house to eat dinner with your extended fam?

What happened to the good old days?

Now we have five locks on the door.

Now I can't even tell you who live right across from me.

Now I get on the elevator I speak, they grunt! WTF is that are we animals?

Forget about eating at your neighbors, you might not make it out alive.

What in the hell happened to the good old days?

Remember when it was okay to drink Kool-Aid and drink tap water?

Remember when it was okay to eat left overs?

Remember when it was okay to eat black-eyed peas, and neck bones, oh and don't forget the cornbread?

Remember when it was okay to wear your sister or brother's hand me down clothes?

Remember the good old days?

Now we are too good for Kool-Aid, it's crystal light in bottle water?

Now finish up that food, because it will go to waste.

Now I don't eat that, it's poor man food, excuse me when in the hell did you become rich?

Now I'm not wearing anything if it did not come out of the store, even if I can't afford it, even if I can't pay my rent, but I'm fly and I paid 300.00 bucks for these jeans.

When in the hell did we become stupid?

We should always remember the time, never forget who you are and where you came from.

I damn sure remember the time, and I am still going through time!

True Confession:
It is good to take your mind back to where you came from at times, just enough to keep you humble and grateful for what you have accomplished.

Loving What You Can't See

I felt you in my womb
But I could not see you
I knew that I loved you
But I could not see you
I felt the butterflies in my stomach
But I could not see you

I enjoyed every minute of trying to
create you
But I could not see you
I watched my body change every day
I felt my nipples expand and my breast change
they changed to a different size a different color
But I could not see you
My belly grew bigger every day
But I could not see you
I carried you with me for months
But I could not see you
That special bond grew stronger and stronger
each day
But I could not see you

The time has come now for you to enter this world
The time has come now for me to see you
I have yearned for this time, this moment
to finally see you, to hold you, to say I love you
The time has come for me to feel and see who is this
person that I have carried for so long
that I have loved and never really met.

On December 1, 1999 at 1:00pm you are here
In my arms, laying on top of me, and all I can
do is stare at you, amazed of the beautiful creation
God has given me, a gift, a gift that will keep on giving
A gift that I can share with my closest friends and family
A gift that will grow and mature, and will give again
The gift of life, the gift of a Baby girl.
This gift that taught me how to love unconditionally!

True Confession:
What can I say. I was happy to carry that life in me and be presented with the most beautiful child ever.

Let's Talk About It!

I want to take a different route on my blog today.

There has been a lot of talk about a certain golf player!

I can't understand for the life of me what the big fuss is about?

Why are we so surprised? This is the life of a Billionaire. It's just like a hustler,

Money, power, and respect, they forgot about the whores, the one who will do anything for that green paper. I can't even say that America respect him, who can respect a man who denies where he come from and who he is. He is accepted not respected.

Pastor Tisdale wrote on his views about this whole situation, he said" this man is an Alpha Male. He has a passion to win." He also said "he is a perfectionist at his game." Well I guess this is one game that he was not good at, the player game.

Many may ask the question why even get married, if you have this driven passion to be on top of everything including another woman other than your wife. I will tell you why, because this is how America the beautiful want it to be. You are a role model, you have to set an example for our children, nope wrong answer! Each and every one of us should be a role model for our own children, and this is a perfect example why! Well I say another one bites the dust! No pity from this end Sir!

True Confession:

I will admit, I was hesitant to write this one, because it is my personal feelings about someone that I really don't know personally, but have been introduced to by the media. Honestly, I can care less about what people do and who they do it with, it's really none of my business. I was just so tired of reports on it. As I said this is not the first and it won't be the last. I was not understanding what the big shock was. In time people will forgive and forget anyway, or will they? Forgiveness is not up to the individual or one self, it is about God.

Another Me

I smile, you say I'm beautiful.
I frown, you ask what's wrong,
I love you, then you open your mouth
you say the wrong thing, now I hate you
Sometimes I wonder is there another me.

You come to me, you tell me your deepest inner thoughts
I want to hear your dreams, your issues, your wishes
I Listen, I give you advice, you value my opinion
You come back again, now I don't want to hear it
You start to complain, you give me a headache,
I tell you not now, I can't do this!
Sometimes I wonder is there another me.

I want you to touch me, taste me, caress me gently
I want you to kiss me, hold me in your arms, where I can feel
safe
I want to explode when you are in me.
Now the moment is gone, it's over, I'm done
Don't touch me, let me go, no I don't want to kiss you every minute of
the day
Sometimes I wonder is there another me.

I like to see your face; I want to wake up with you
I want to have breakfast with you every morning
I want us to go to the park, I want to travel to the other side of the
world with you
I want us to become one, man and woman, husband and wife.
Now I'm tired, you are smothering me, I feel like I'm walking with
shackles on my ankles, I want to be free
I want you to get off of me

I need the key, the key to unlock these shackles, I want to be," free to be me".
Damn now I know there is another side of me, or maybe it's just where
I always wanted to be Just Free!

True Confession:
*This seems to be me in a relationship that I really didn't want. I really want
to say this is menopause, but it was way too early for that. At times I wanted
the flesh, but not the emotional part that came with the relationship. There
are many times in my life where I settled for less, when I really should have
just moved on.*

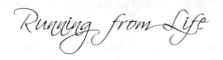

Running from Life

Sometimes living in this world is like a mouse
Living in a maze.
You keep going and going, but not finding your way.
Each time you hit a road, there's a wall there to block you,
Or at least that's what you say.
You're running from life.

Sometimes living in this world is like a butterfly in a cocoon
Just waiting for that perfect moment to bloom
But wait, there's a struggle, you lose a wing, you can't find
Your way out, now what do you do?
You keep fighting, or do you give up and die, you never have the opportunity
To fly.
You're running from life.

Sometimes living in this world is so rough and tough
You just want to give it all up
You have food to eat, you have a roof over your head
Even better you have a job, but you still can't take it
It's not enough, you want more, give me, give me is all you know
Now you lose it, because you were too ungrateful to
Appreciate what you had, it's gone what do you do?
You're running from life.

Sometimes this road we travel is not easy
Sometimes you will get lost
Sometimes you just want to turn back and say fuck it I give up
But what is life if you don't learn how to live?
What is life if there are no trouble times?

You keep running from instead of running for and you will never
Find your way,
You can't run from life, nor can you let it run you!

True Confessions:
*This is another favorite of mine. Life will come at you with some heavy shit.
It's not about what is coming, but more about how do you deal with it. Life
has not been smooth sailing for many of us, but we find a way to make it,
I know I have. I have learned not to ask why, but how. How do I take on
this challenge and come out winning on the other side?*

Heaven or Hell?

Ok, this will be different. I am about to touch something that is taken
Very seriously, and I guess it should be.
I have always wondered about Heaven and Hell
Is there such a physical place?
The church teaches us that there is, but when you think about it how
can that be?
How can Hell be right below us?
How can I walk the earth and not feel this hot place under my feet?
Just think on a hot summer day, you can feel that sun blast on your ass
You can feel that sun all in your faces, rays so high, that it will turn
Your skin a different color.
I ask you this, how many miles away is the sun from earth? Yes, I know,
but I want you to think
For those who want to think

What about that great place in the sky? That place they call Heaven.
Ok man has been to the moon and back.
I have flown above the clouds many of times
Where are those pearly gates?
Where is this fine place in the sky?

Now don't get me wrong I love my Jesus
But I'm also a realist, and for real
Heaven and Hell has to be a condition
A state of mind
I have my heaven and hell right here on earth
Some days can be Heaven, and others straight Hell!

Now don't go getting all fired up over this, I am only expressing my opinion.
Wow, only if my mother would read this one!

True Confession:

This something that I have thought about plenty of times. I took more a philosophical approach on this piece. I was not trying to disrespect anyone or rub people the wrong way, I just want people to think outside of the box. Stop thinking from what you have been taught all of your life, but try thinking on your own. Here is another question to ponder, how many people that have passed on came back to tell you about Heaven or Hell?

These Walls

What is about these walls?
I see you, we meet, we talk, we vibe
You get to know me; I get to know you.
By now you know just about my life story, so I let you in
I let you into my space, my walls

You were knocking at the door, I hesitated because I was not sure
of how you would feel once you were in
knowing what could happen, so I open the door and let you in
You come in, you greet me with a kiss, but you seem a little afraid,
afraid of what the outcome may be
I give you a gesture to let you know that it's okay,
it's okay for you to continue to get to this room,
this room with comfort, this room with these walls,
these walls that can keep you warm

So you are here in the room,
you enter real slow and careful, you are really gentle with your entrance
as you come in I can feel something
I can feel this chemistry that runs all through my body
Wow! What is that?
You look into my eyes, and I look into yours
you don't say much out your mouth, but I'm reading your eyes,
and your eyes are telling me that you like the surrounding of these walls
that you are in, the warmth, the wetness, the tightness that wrap itself
around you
You like how the walls make you feel
These walls can sometimes feel like they are closing in on you,
but you seem to enjoy the company and feeling.

Damn! What is it about these walls?

Why do you keep coming back into these walls?

These walls that make you feel so special and so warm on the inside.

You tell me you love me because of these walls that I let you in?

Or is it me and my presence? Is it the beauty that you see on the outside?

Or is it what you are feeling on the inside?

Now you tell me where are you?

What is this place?

What is it about these special walls that make you never want to leave?

True Confession:

I wanted to add a little sexiness to my writings. Yep "these walls" can be that sexual place or it can be a sexy ass room that a person is in. Allow this to take your mind where ever you see fit and feel free.

Free dumb of Speech

Free dumb of speech is what I like to call it
Do you really believe you are free to speak?
Do you really believe that there won't be repercussions if you say the wrong thing?
Free dumb of speech is what I like to call it

Yes, they say we are not slaves
Yes, they say we are free
Yes, they say we can go where we please
Yes, they say we can love who we want to love
Yes, they say we can hate who we want to hate
But think about all these things, who do you work for?
What do you say out your mouth and who do you say it to?
Travel to another side of the world without proper papers and see if your ass get back!
Love that white man, white girl, same sex, opposite races, and see how they treat you
Tell your boss (master) how you really feel and you will see how free you are
Free dumb of speech is what I like to call it

I would be a fool to believe I am anywhere near free is this country
The only freedom is my internal freedom, and the freedom to write
The freedom to allow what is on my heart to flow through my veins and leak out the
Pen that I hold in my hand.
This is Freedom, this is where I am Free to be Me!

True Confession:
I heard it said that America is the land of the free and brave. Maybe, there is some truth to this, there may be some Brave folks roaming this place, but not so free. The system has a way of controlling everything that we

as a people can do and say. I understand rules and regulations, but they should be for everyone with no exceptions. We live in a place where it is okay to have a President who is openly racist, sexist, narcissistic and the list of "ist" can go on and on. I am only free in my mind, because I know who I am and I know the world that we live in. Do I understand? No, not at all and I don't believe the world will change.

Not Good Enough

They say I'm not good enough!
They say my hair is too nappy
My lips are too big
My skin is too dark
Why are your eyes so brown?

They say I'm not good enough!
They say my ass is too big
My feet are too large
Damn I'm not good enough!

They say I'm too strong
They say they don't like my attitude
They say they don't like my tight fitting jeans
that show every curve on my body
They say I'm not good enough!

I say I am more than enough!
I say you can't handle me
I say you can't handle how I sway my hips
and my ass across the floor
How I have your man or lady looking and wanting more
I say you can't handle how I can style my
nappy hair any way I please
and do that shit with pleasure and ease
I say you can't handle my juicy lips and
the words that massage your ears when I speak!
So I believe you love what you see
You sitting there trying to figure out how to be me

You know what else I say?
I say I love me and who the Fuck are they any way!
They don't know me! I'm more than enough!

True Confession:
This is based on other races being so judge mental of the Black woman.
For many years' society has portrayed the image of Beautiful should be
and how it should look. I have learned to love who I am and embrace
my Beauty along with any flaws I may think I have. Never allow no one
to tell you how you should really look and feel about yourself. Always
love you!

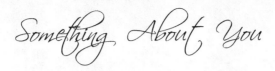

Something About You

It's Something about you, that made me stare at you

It's something about you, that made me want to know you better

It's something about you, that made me forget about the rules

It's something about you, that made me feel so comfortable that I could show you my bare skin

It's something about you, that made me forget about how you would treat me after allowing you to taste my goodies

It's something about you, that had me travel many many miles to see you

It's something about you, that makes me feel good when you are not even touching me, when I can't see you, nor even hear you

I can still feel you, but you never touched me, I can hear you, but you never talked to me, It's something about you

It's something about you, that makes me want to kiss you

Damn what is it about you?

Na! I'm not open, it's just something about you that keeps me wondering!

True Confession:

I have a feeling I know who this is about, one of my fantasy relationship that wasn't really a relationship, it was all about the flesh. This is about someone who I can't say too much about right now. I would call it a fling that probably shouldn't have happened. I live life with no regrets and enjoyed every moment of this fling at the time. It was just something about him that caught my eye.

My Brother's Keeper

You didn't want me around when I came out our mother's womb,
You sat and watched while I almost killed myself
We fought every chance we got, I tried to take you away from here.
Am I my brother's keeper?
You never said you loved me
You never even hugged me
You never really wanted me around, what is this?
Am I my brother's keeper?
We are older now, you leave to go away, I cry what is this?
Am I my brother's keeper?
Some time has passed we are grown now, I don't see you much but I miss you like crazy. What is this?
Am I my brother's keeper?
I ask you what's up, you tell me you love from a distance, what is this?
You say you have been hurt by the ones who were supposed to love you, the man who was my father, what is this? How can they do this? You stayed around for me, to protect me, and was not telling me that you really did love me.
Damn who is my brother's keeper?

True Confession:
This piece is about my biological brother. Some Families have dark secrets that they like to sweep under the rug and keep it moving. The belief of there is healing in time, may be true to an extinct. This case it took many years of healing and praying for my brother and him finding his own therapy to help him through the rough times. I was too young to realize what was going on and what happened to my brother, that I will not share in this book or ever in life. I do know that my brother loves me and he loved me then. I remember the day when he expressed to me what was going on with him as a child, I wish there

was something that I could do, other than cry. I was at work reading an email that he sent to me and I felt like someone put their hand in my chest and ripped my heart out. I sat in the locker room at my job and cried, feeling lifeless and helpless. I could only say that I was so sorry this happened to him and I am sorry for any violent abuse that my Dad may have caused him. I can't bring this up to anyone in my family, because my brother has made peace with the situation and he forgives them for any harm they have brought to him. I also forgive them for hurting my brother and I am glad that we have the connection that we have right now. A conversation, an apology would have been the right thing to do, because you know what was done, but remember God sees all and he knows all, yes he is a forgiving God also. I am grateful that he saved a person like me. God has changed my heart and my way of thinking many years ago.

My Reality

Love Not Lust
Obligation not Oblivious
Your Dedication and Determination
Adherence not Advantage
Liability not Lack of
Trust not Turmoil
Your Faithfulness

Now tell me who you Loyal to?

The Most High God!

True Confession:
loy·al·ty
/ˈloiəltē/

noun

1. the quality of being loyal.
    "her **loyalty to** her husband of 34 years"
○   a strong feeling of support or allegiance.
    plural noun: **loyalties**
    "fights with in-laws are distressing because they cause **divided loyalties**"

At times I wonder if people know the true definition of loyalty. I gave my understanding of loyalty and what it means to me and then gave the dictionary version of it. I believe that people don't have any loyalty to each other or to themselves and this is how so many relationships fail. This is just my opinion. I believe in order for one to really be loyal to another person, they need to first be loyal to themselves, which goes back to the statement of loving yourself and knowing who you are.

The question of loyalty popped in my mind after going through an unsuccessful marriage, I asked myself if he really understood loyalty. I won't go into any other details, because this is not to bash anyone at all, but just to give my perspective on how I was feeling at the time. I have prayed for healing and I am in a good place right now.

Soul Food

Mouth salivating, aroma of warm hot buttered bread
Making my body feel good, with the thought of cornbread in my head
Cast iron, stainless steel, corning ware, they all hold enough that can be shared
Only if I could take a piece, have a small taste
Momma yells Get out my pots before I slap your face
This food is good for my soul

Collard Greens, Potato Salad, Fried Chicken, Mac and Cheese and candied yams,
Momma can I have some more Please, Please, Please, Oh Damn!
Bananas peeled and sliced, milk for the pudding, vanilla wafers, sugar and whipped egg whites
This is a desert that I more than like, this is a dish that when I eat goes straight to my lovely hips
Banana pudding leave a sweet creamy taste on my lips
Oh this food is good for my soul

Grease is hot, sizzling and steady, fish is seasoned and ready, drop it in the pan oh so deep,
Golden brown as it rises to the top and float around
Put that on my plate, I want to sit and watch the "Get down"
Oh this food is good for my soul

Sliced ham and Fried Fat back, now you know you are not supposed to eat that
Pork chops and pigs' feet all the things that will make your heart skip several beats
Now you better run, you better run and get away from that bad ass meat
All that food was good for your soul, now may you forever rest in peace.

True Confession:

Generation after generation, all the way back to slavery, black families were taught to eat what they had to survive. It took a whole lot of hypertension, diabetes and heart failure for some to realize the high sodium affordable food was killing us slowly. Don't get me wrong I enjoyed a lot of this food and still do this day. I learned to have things in moderation and as a treat, in order for me to stay healthy. I definitely don't eat pork anymore and have not touched it for about 20 years or more. This piece expressed how good food made me feel and how the smell of it cooking was so soothing and satisfying to my soul. There is nothing better than a good home cooked meal. I thank my parents for showing me around in the kitchen.

Tears of Joy

Compassion, Content, Complete and Complacent
Smiling, Serene, Sensual and Sensitive
Your scent, your eyes, your walk and your style
Lead to a Love that will last for an everlasting while

Tears of Joy
The touch from you hand
The kiss from your lips
The exotic words from your mouth
All tell me you are not a boy

Tears of Joy
Excited, Happy, Joyous, blithe
This is a feeling that may seem like a myth
Finally, I can cleanse my soul
Feeling like I have reached the ultimate goal
No fear, No sadness, No pain
Tears of Joy and Love is what I have gain

True Confession:
When writing this piece, I was stuck for a moment on how to really express what tears of joy mean to me personally. I had a hard time explaining it, because I have not felt this before other than when I was having a personal moment with God, at least that is what I thought. I then realized how I have shed tears, when I completed my degree, when I gave birth to my child, when I got divorced instead of when I got married. Then when I met the Love of my life, most recently, Yes, "Tears of Joy" is a beautiful feeling.

TB and ME

1991 is where it begin
A time in my life where
I thought it would end

I have done what I was
Supposed to do,
So why come in my life
And take over as if I
Belong to you

Parties, pleasures, prestige & positive attitude
Sat deep in my soul like a hot stew,
All of this until the moment
I encountered you

Lump on my neck, bald spot in my head,
Curves in my body depleted,
I'm feeling half dead

Isoniazid, Rifampin, & Ethambutol,
I had to ingest, and take them all with
A burning and clogged up chest

From Exposed to Class III from a smear
It really didn't matter
And I really didn't care
What I didn't think about has now become my biggest fear

Now I sit for years trying
To figure out why, wondering will I ever forget,
Will I tell this mess goodbye?

Now I get it, now I see
This whole situation
Is a minor reflection of me

Now I get it, now I see
This relationship between TB & ME
You see it's not about me at all,
God used me so that I can uplift
And make sure the next man doesn't fall

True Confessions:
As a very young adult I was diagnosed with Tuberculosis. I woke up one morning and discovered a swollen lymph node. I did not understand what was happening to me. I did not feel any sickness, I was not coughing, no pain in my chest, no fevers, just this ugly lump. I went to the hospital. I was asked a series of questions in regards to my work and who I lived with, if I traveled out of the country. Finally, I was given a PPD test, which wasted no time in flaring up 4ccm's, indicating a positive result. I then became very concerned and confused as to what and how did I get this disease. I recall the Dr. telling me that I had been exposed to TB. I had no way of finding out who I contracted this disease from. I had to have a surgery to remove the excess tissue and fluid from my lymph node and have it sent to the lab for further testing. This disease attempted to take control of my body. I was already very slim and lost weight along with losing my hair over night from taking the medication. I was on medication for 9 complete months and now if I get tested I will always show as positive. When I was accepted to study and work with the HRTP at DOHMH and was placed in Tuberculosis department many years later, I knew this was God placing me there and I had to find another way to help others and spread the word of the importance for finding a cure. I was told that I had to be around someone with the disease constantly in order for me to get it, this is not true. During this time, I was living with my mother who was working in health care and she did not have it. After further investigation, I found out that I was not simply exposed, but I had the actual disease.

With faith a prayer I was able to make it through and for that I am forever grateful. I was able to speak at two engagements for DOHMH Department of Health and Mental Hygiene, and help others spread the word. I will always be willing to tell my story, because you never know how it may help the next person to overcome their own battle.

Harlem

Harlem you have always been a friend of mine
Even back then when calls were just a dime
I walked these streets with grace and time
Always had Harlem on my mind

Harlem you have always been a friend of mine
You gave me culture and a sense of pride
Where the girls looked like me
And the brothers were oh so fine
Block parties, water pumps and sprinklers, had us on some cool shit
All of this with a fresh pair of kicks

Harlem you have always been a friend of mine
A place where I could grow
Walked these streets and talked to people I didn't know
Sun beaming on my face giving it a kiss
No worries about what I will miss

Harlem you have always been a friend of mine
The streets that were known as the hood
And helping a sister out was all good
This is a place that kept me wrapped in its arms
And loved me with its charm

Harlem born, Harlem strong, a place where I see no wrong
Harlem you will always be a friend of mine…

True Confession:
Harlem is where I was actually born and raised. I was born at St. Luke's Hospital on 114th and Amsterdam and was raised from 149th st and 8th avenue to 155th st. 8th avenue, Polo Ground Towers. I grew up during

a time where it was a little rough, but the communities looked out for one another and it gave us a sense of security and thick skin. Harlem also gave us a sense of pride, from the way we dressed to how we styled our hair. There was something that was always different about Harlem, some of the best came from Harlem. For example; Langston Hughes, Zora Neale Hurston, W.E.B. DuBois and the list can go on. I am very proud to be who I am and where I come from. I hope that I become and legacy and an inspiration to others who want to write or be artist.

Good Morning World

Can I take a moment and introduce you to me?
Good Morning World is what I like to say,
But people will judge and call me cra-cra

Good Morning World
Is all I want to say
But we live in a world full of hate, selfishness and shame
People will turn their head the other way

As I walk through this place called life
And look at the faces around me
The faces that supposed to be beautiful
I wonder, I sit and think what did you have on your plate last night
Did you have envy, greed and a side of hate

Good Morning World
We live in a world where a boy wants to be a girl
And a girl wants to be a boy, and they still can't find no joy
There is no joy because of fear of judgement,
Judgement from those who quote a book that was written by man
Judgment from those who say they love all
But will disown you when you fall

Good Morning World
We are here in this place that is lead through pure hate
We are here in this place where love is used to cover up and not comfort
the soul
We are in this place where being in love is just boring and old

Good Morning World is what I want to say
Helping is what I want to do,
Sharing is in my heart, but there are those who will rip that apart

Good Morning World! Good Morning World! I said Good Morning World!
Putting my pen to the paper and letting my blood flow again

True Confession:

Have you ever walked into a room in the morning and say Good Morning and people don't really respond, or you get a grunt? Or, you get on the elevator at work and say Good Morning and no one open their mouth? You ever observe people on the NYC train and walking the street, they are barely smiling. I wonder if ever day of everyone's life is that bad? I wonder if people really have any joy within them. I spoke a little bit about transgender population, not in a negative light, but to shine light on such a difficult topic. I am a person who truly love all, I don't care who you are as long as you are kind, true and honest with me I will deliver that same energy to you. I have gay family members and I love them no matter what anyone else have to say. God did not put us here to judge one another. I know some will read this and may get a little annoyed, but please keep an open mind and know these are my opinions and my truth, nothing here is based on fact.

Who Am I?

When you look at me who do you see?
Am I the woman that you thought I would be?
Sit still and listen to me,
and I can show you Who God intended for me to be.

Who am I?
I don't want you to look around me.
It's not about how society has made me up to be
It's only about what you see.
Put your hand in my hand and take this ride with me
And trust and believe you will love me for me.

Who am I?
I wish I could be like you,
The strong, the one who stand tall,
The one who held the torch and
Promised to pick me up when I fall.
But that is not me, I am not that statue in the middle of the station,
The one who seems like he is holding up the whole damn nation,
I am just that woman, who want to always be your motivation.

Who am I?
Let me take a moment and introduce me to you.
No, I refuse to be called your Boo,
See a Boo is young and don't know exactly what to do.
I am a woman, a mother, a sister, a friend, that true one
Who will really be there in the end.
I have been a wife, a teacher, more like an educator,

Who really have little time for the perpetrator.

Who am I?
When you see me, there should be no fog,
Let your mind be clear and understand, I will nurture the kids and the dog.
I am that one, who will lift you up, when your head is in the sand,
And will still understand and respect you as a man.

Who am I?
Please, don't lay there with your face looking like the clouds in the sky,
I know this world have you ask the question why
I can see that you are confused and blue, but you can trust and believe
I know what to do.

Who am I?
I am that woman that many want to be, the one who has her hand in everything.
The one who can do it all, and rarely does she trip and fall.
Oh, trust and believe this didn't happen overnight
I had to put on my gloves and fight.

Who am I?
I am that sparrow that I wear on my back,
I wear him with pride because he is the one who get me through this ride.
He represents me, a woman who is free!
Free to love God, my family, and more importantly,
Free to love ME! This is who I am!

True Confession:
I did this piece with in mind of something like the Introduction to me, but instead this goes a little bit deeper, with who I am and how I feel about the perception of me. Some people will look at me and pass judgement without taking the time to get to know me. Sometimes, you have to step back and evaluate who you really are. I live in a world where I have been judge by the color of my skin, or where I live and work. At the end of the day, who am I, I am a woman of God and in my opinion there is nothing stronger than that.

Letter to My Daddy

Dear Daddy,

I only can wish and dream that you were still here to see how life has taken a turn for your baby girl. I am now 37 yrs. old, with a beautiful daughter. I wish that you were here to see her. Well daddy I must say that this life for me has not been easy, especially in the love area, but there is one thing that you taught me and that was to love myself first. A lot of times I can hear your voice in my head when I am going through some nonsense with a man. I can remember you always saying "Hey listen! Don't worry everything is going to be alright." You have never lied about that, I have learned that in due time everything will eventually be alright. Daddy I want to thank you for teaching me how to cook. I still don't have it as good as you, but I do get a lot of special request. Guess what Daddy! I remember how you taught me to make homemade stuffing and a really good turkey, I was able to share that experience with my co-workers this year. Yes, that is right I cooked a really good turkey and they really enjoyed it. It was almost like you were right there in the kitchen with me all over again, guiding me and telling me what to do. You taught me how to cook to taste without any measurements, but just by knowing. Thank you so much for that. Daddy, I know that you did not play a big role in my schooling education, but you did teach me many life lessons in a placid way. Like the very first time you ever admitted to me that you had a drinking problem. That taught me that it is okay to ask for help never have too much pride, because pride will only hold you back from moving forward. I remember the phone call like it was just yesterday, that you were in the hospital again, but I never knew that would be the last time I would see you alive. There is so much that I should have said to you then. Like thank you, thank you for always loving me and teaching me to love my daughter the way that you loved me, but even better, to make sure that I take care of myself, so that I can be here on earth with her as long as possible. Thank you daddy, for introducing me to that mean disease called AIDS. You never told me anything about it, but I was able to see it face to face when I looked at you lying on your death bed. Daddy I do understand, you wanted to protect my feelings as usual, and so I thank you for that. This has all been a life lesson to me; I know exactly what to do and what not to do. Daddy there are no hard feelings, for whatever it is worth I just want to thank you for the time we did have here together and the life lessons.

Love,
Versalle (your image)

True Confession:
This was written, with the thought of if I could talk to my Dad what would I say to him. My Dad passed away when I was 23 years old, which was before I was married and before I had my daughter. Every year, even up until now 2020, whenever my Father's birthday come around I become heartbroken all over again. The pain of losing a loved one never heal, you learn to live without them, but will forever miss them. My father left me with so many unanswered questions. Now, the only thing that I can do is carry my great memories of him and the Love he left me with. I share this deep Love with my daughter and family.

Let Me Introduce Myself

Hi let Me introduce Myself.

Forget about my name and who you see on the outside.

Take a good look at what is on the inside.

I have a heart that you can't see with the human eye, but if you get close enough to me you can feel my heart beat.

You will learn that there is a different rhythm.

You see I am not your average pretty face and pretty smile.

I am that one that you will call on in your time of need.

You can call me friend and know that it is real. I am that one who really use my ears to listen, and speak when it is necessary.

See I don't use these lips to judge or put you down, I will be the one to give you my hand when you fall to the ground, and if you are too heavy for me to hold up, I will just get two pillows and a blanket and we will lay there together until we can figure this one out.

I am that one that will be by your side in the belly of the beast.

I will help you to believe, that we are to fear no man except God!

I am that woman who cry when you cry, or who can be strong and just wipe your tears away, and say I know we will be okay.

See most people think they know me but they really don't.

Again let Me Introduce Myself.

Hi I am an amazing Beautiful Black Woman, with a mind that is so powerful and always in control of my body, and my decisions.

I am a woman who loves education, and will always keep myself open for a great learning experience.

I will never tell you that I know, because I don't know! I am just learning!

I don't look for love, because I have Love!

Now my question to you is, now that you have met me, will you allow me to share my Love with you? There is always space in my heart for loving real people!

True Confession:

Introduction to who I am is similar to "Who Am I" but with less of a poet flow. This piece will give you an idea of who I am and my Love for Love. This is about being true to myself and to others.

Still Standing

Hello he said to me
You are as pretty as pretty can be

Hello he said to me
What is your name?
You are not the average kind of dame
Beautiful you are
If you walk away
My heart will have a scar

Hello he said to me
Let's hang out
I will treat you right without a doubt
Don't be afraid skip school
Forget about those grades
Let me teach you something new

Hello he said to me
If you trust and take my hand
I will love you and be your man

Hello I said to him
Little did I know how this would end
You were never my friend
You touched me No I said
You touched me again No I said

Hello I said to him
Never knew this would change my life
It would have been better to stab me with a knife
You took what wasn't yours

I guess you thought you hit a high score
You became a face I hated more and more
My relief would not turn to grief
I became happy when your life came to an end
I saw this as my biggest revenge
Now I ask God to forgive me for my own sin
This is where your life end and mine begin

Hello is forever Goodbye
For these feelings have died

True Confession:
I wrote this not looking for sympathy or even understanding as to why people do what they do to others. No I am not of the "me too" movement. I just finally found a way to express what I kept as a secret for so many years. People ask why wouldn't someone say something during the time it happened. I can only speak for myself and what I was feeling at the time. I left school to go hang out with a boy in his house, what would my mother really think? Would she believe my story? I was in a place where I was not supposed to be. This would get all around in the school and I would have a bad name, because this is clearly my fault. Yes, I blamed myself for being irresponsible and at the same time trusting someone who I thought I knew. I put this situation in a far memory bank, so far back that I can't remember too many of the details of that day. I found the courage to share this information many years later when I received a phone call saying that he was killed. I became emotionless, no response, no remorse, I felt a sense of relief that he was gone, figuring that is another memory I could completely erase and find closure.

I will say this too all woman and men who have been violated in their life, please don't be afraid to talk to someone about it. I made a poor choice of not speaking to anyone until, many years later. There is nothing wrong with seeking professional help.

Covid19

Quarantine, what does this all mean
Is this a way to drive us all insane or to show us how to be clean
Quarantine what does this all mean, how do we deal with something
that was a cruel idea,
Is this a sick way to install in us fear
Quarantine what does this all mean
Will this teach us all how to be true human beings
Covid19 is a virus that feel like a mean dis ease
What do you mean stay home, stay away, keep to yourself
Learn to love and deal with yourself, before you can come back out and
deal with the world
Covid19 is not a nice friend to me
I know this is not the end or the way God want it to be
Tickle in the throat, cough, sneeze and high fever, unable to breathe
with ease
Hospitalized and put on a machine
Where is the most High, ask the ones who don't believe
I need to find the God in me
Quarantine what does it all mean
Days turn to weeks, weeks turn to months, how do I learn to adjust again
Will I always have doubts and fear or will I come out on the other end
stronger and better
Or will any of this even matter
Quarantine what does this all mean
Me for you and you for me, we will always have a shoulder to lean on
But she just might teach me how to love you more and to embrace all
of me.

True Confession:

I am sitting here the 5th day of Covid19 Quarantine lock down and it is really allowing me to think about life and what all of this mean to me. I have no proof, but I do have Faith and know that God has spared my life and brought me very far. I know he does not want it to all end like this, but I do believe he is trying to get someone's attention. I have been paying attention a long time ago. This is a perfect opportunity for rest and reconnection with our loved ones. Think about how many times you speak to your family and friends that don't live with you. It's always, I have to do this, or I have to work, or I don't have time to do that right now. Well now we all have the time that we could not find to reflect on the "what if". I will continue to write and focus on my future plans, with faith that this will all pass and lessons will be learned. Peace and blessings to everyone.

Connection

There is a bridge one that is old but Beautiful

Especially when the night fall and the lights

Hit the reflection off the water

So close but so far

Separated by this bridge

A bridge I fear to cross

As I may fall when I pass through

True Confession:
I wrote this piece in 2018, not sure where my emotions were during this time, but I believe I was having a fear of allowing someone in my space at that time. I know I was going through my divorce at that time and trying to hold it all together at the time. Depression did kick in during this time and I was not trusting many people, especially men at this time. It was difficult to connect with anyone.

Here We Go Again

Here we go again
You sound like Biz, "This Girl Is only a Friend"
Let's go back to where this shit began
Back to the beginning when I wanted it to end

Here we go again
You call this chic a friend
Mountain Melons sit on top
You look at them and maybe say "don't stop"
You protect her as if she is your own, as if she is not fully aware and grown

Here we go again
The pain, the tears, the fears
When I believed this shit was in the rear

Here we go again
I said Here we go again
Where is my Love, where is my friend?
Where is my King who said he will love me until the end?

Here we F@$%ing go again!
I look in the mirror and see I am my only friend.

True Confession:
On 11/27/2017 my ex-husbands birthday, after 4 years of re-marriage and almost 23 years in my life, I found out that he was apparently interested in another young lady, (my version of cheating on me). Everyone have their own definition of cheating, my opinion, not a fact, is if you are with someone in a committed relationship, your attention should not be on someone else. This does not mean that you can't have friends, but there are certain boundaries which should not be crossed. I

will not go any further with this, because I have passed this time in my life, but as you can see I was hurt, really hurt. I finally made the decision to end it all and file for a divorce. This is not to male bash or even speak negative about him, we tried and it didn't work out as planned, he is just not my forever and I am not his. We are now friends and get along as we should. He is an amazing Dad and I Love him for that alone.

Sleepless Nights

Why put up a fight?
Toss and turn, my mind is full of crazy thoughts
Something is not right

Television, Internet, Cooking, Reading, Eating, working from home online
All of this to occupy what seems like nothing but useless time
It becomes more and more difficult to clear my head and take this heavy
world off my mind

Walk to the window
Walk to the kitchen
Searching for a way out
Something to satisfy my empty feeling of space and time
Afraid to walk outside
My skin in 2020 with no grace and no mercy seems to be a crime
How do I get back what is rightfully mine?
How do I move on and erase this awful memory this horrendous time?

Just when I learned to love what I can't see
My Faith, My Belief, My God and the Beauty in me
Here comes this invisible, mysterious phantom of dis ease
Trying to twist my mind completely
Take away my breathe, my courage and my dignity
Feeling like the only friend I have is the reflection that I can see

Sleepless nights I may have many
Quarantine taught me to have a new love for life and the friend in me
May this time pass soon and our new lives may resume

True Confession:

We are living in new times and crucial times. At times people may take the simple things in life for granted, like slowing down and appreciating your home and family time. People have spent too much time focused on materialistic things in life and entertainment. Living in New York which is overpriced, really focused on all the wrong things, people rush to work, over crowd the subways, knock you down if you are in their walking space, or don't know the meaning of personal space at all. It is unfortunate that a deadly virus had to show some of us what life should really be about, respecting space and time. Take a time out to get to know yourself and who you really are. This is a new journey that will not be easy for anyone and we will have sleepless nights, but never give up and hold on to your faith.

Tomiko Brown

Beautiful, Bold, Bodacious is this Beloved Lady
Daughter, Mother, Grandmother, Sister and Friend if
you have Tomiko Brown in your life you Win!
Uniqueness begins with her name and her
style and she is far from a game
Oh yes she can be feisty and fierce at the same damn time,
but will still have your back at the drop of a dime
Soft and Sweet she can be if you really open your eyes you will see
There's another side to her where she will allow
you to be whoever you want to be
No judgement, acumen or discernment, a friend that
will build a bond that won't break or bend
You damn right I call Tomiko Brown my Best Friend!
Best Friend she is more than that to me, she is my sister,
my therapist and my mentor all at the same time
I know I have a shoulder to lean on as well as she has mine

Never selfish or egocentric, she carries the world on her shoulders
and back, anything she do you will know she truly meant it
Tomiko Brown will always be a friend of mine
She could write my life story and I can tell you hers every single time
I have no fear of her every betraying me, because
honest is all she knows how to be
I know she is my friend and I am hers and this is why we both Win!

True Confession:

I was introduced to this woman many years ago by our other Best Friend (J. Mac is who I will call her, because I did not get permission to use her name, but everybody knows who she is). We were called "three the hard way" when we were younger because you could not separate us. Over the years we continued our relationship which easily became a sisterhood. Tomiko asked me some years back when I started writing to do a piece for her. I said I would, but never took the time to do it. These words express exactly what I feel for her over the years. She is the God Mother to my daughter and has been by my side through some very rough times in my life. I am not sure why I picked this particular year (2020) to do this for her 49th birthday, but my Spirit told me to do it. I will never forget when my Mother was 1st diagnosed with Cancer and fell ill in her home and was not able to walk. My mother had a horrible bowel accident in her diaper and I was trying to clean her, before the ambulance came to take her to the hospital, but between the sadness in my Mother's eyes and the sickening smell, I was not able to handle it. Tomiko stepped right in as if my Mother's was her own Mother and cleaned her up for me. The list can go on about the things she has done for me and the relationship that we have built over the years. True friendship and sisterhood is hard to find, so I cherish my relationships/ friendships.

Tyson Hall

Classic Man, Gentleman, Angel, Saint even a Gem, the list can
go on, but most of all Tyson is the true meaning of a Friend
Talented, Diplomatic, Artistic one of a kind, not
like most men Tyson is better than fine wine
Dedicated, Determined and so Ambitious that one may
look at his style and his ways and become Suspicious
Listen Beloved don't be a fool by judging what
you don't understand, that's just not cool
Sit back relax and watch this man, allow him
to educate you and take you to school
No, don't be reluctant, unsure or afraid, step into his
space and you will realize a true man has been made
Tyson Hall a true meaning of a Friend
He will be good to you from the beginning until the end
From a Father to his children and a son to his mother, God
knew what he was doing when he created this brother.
Tyson Hall an original man that make you want
to walk and talk with him again and again
Never Forget Tyson is the true meaning of a Friend!

True Confession:

I have known Tyson for about 30 years or more. We went to high school
together. I remember him in school just as I described him in this
piece. Tyson and I never got the chance to get to know each other on
a serious personal level, I am not sure why, I guess it was not our time,
but I will admit I was always attracted to him and very much drawn
to his personality and always wanted to get to know him better. I held
Tyson at a higher level from the other guys in the school. Tyson to me
was that Dude, just a cool person to know and have good conversation
with. I had a different level of respect for Tyson Hall and I still do now.

I have the pleasure and honor to spend a little more time with Tyson on another level and I can truly say, he is just who I believed he was and even better than I imagined. Tyson is the one who encouraged me to pursue my dream of writing my book. I was sitting on this for 10 years now. When I told Tyson that I love poetry and I love to free write he immediately began to push me in the direction of publishing and sharing my work with the world. Tyson told me that I have a talent and I should be sharing it with the world. Thank you for your encouragement and Inspiration. Thank you for being the charming, intelligent, caring and loving man that you are.

M.B.

I'm not the man you vision me to be
Let me explain what the initials really mean to me
Strength, Struggle, Satisfying, Scholarly is all in me, and when I
speak with you I leave you in a place only one can imagine to be
Let's be clear, you think you know M.B.
But sit still, give me your ear and listen attentively
A Hustler, A Tough Guy and a Lady Lover is
all the shit your vision appeared to see
I can tell you that's not the real me

Entrepreneur, Educated, Elevated, Earnest and Eager
All the things many wish they had the desire to achieve
And if it hurt you to hear what I am saying,
please do me the honor and leave
No, No, No, don't get this misconstrued
And please don't be a fool; I am far from nasty or trying to be rude

I want you to look pass your vision and look at me
I want you to pay close attention to the real M.B.
A distinguished, loving and caring kind of man
The one who when you fall will always reach out his hand
I'm not like many men
When you are allowed in my space you have no doubt
that I am a friend and you are in the right place

No M.B. is not your average man
He is not one to guess, but knows that he can
He knows that M.B. means more than Mike Boogie
M.B. means much better, which is where you would be
if you took a moment to get to know the real me!

Created by V. Shelton 2-14-2018

True Confession:

I have known Michael Hollingsworth aka Mike Boogie, for what seems like forever. We met way back in Junior High School. We disconnected over many years, well he had to go through life and so did I. We were able to reconnect through Social Media a few years back and grew close and remained friends as if we never disconnected. Michael has always been a person that I could call on for any situation. As he like to say "when the bat signal goes up and it's you, I am there". That is a great feeling to know that you have people like that in your life, actually it is a blessing and I am grateful. This piece was done because I know his story, and I know where he has been and who he is now is not the man he was. I never referred to him as "Mike Boogie", because that was always a person that I didn't really care for, but I always knew that he had so much more to offer in life and when I had the opportunity to listen to him speak, I heard and saw exactly what I always knew. Mr. Michael Hollingsworth was just waiting to come out. Thank you for staying true to yourself and true to me.

CPSIA information can be obtained
at www.ICGtesting.com
Printed in the USA
BVHW032016290920
589920BV00002B/21/J